P9-EEJ-201

LAND O LAKES

Cookie COLLECTION

LAND O LAKES™
Cookie COLLECTION

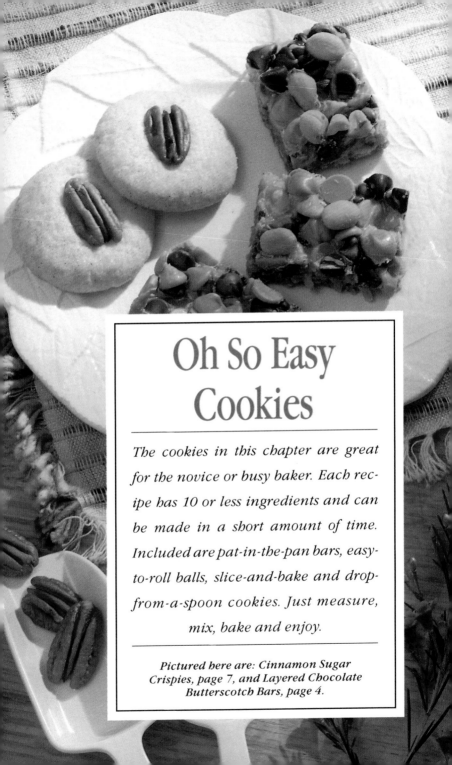

Oh So Easy Cookies

The cookies in this chapter are great for the novice or busy baker. Each recipe has 10 or less ingredients and can be made in a short amount of time. Included are pat-in-the-pan bars, easy-to-roll balls, slice-and-bake and drop-from-a-spoon cookies. Just measure, mix, bake and enjoy.

Pictured here are: Cinnamon Sugar Crispies, page 7, and Layered Chocolate Butterscotch Bars, page 4.

SOUR CREAM CHERRY BARS

Cool and creamy—these cherry bars are topped with crunchy almonds.

Crust
- 2 cups all-purpose flour
- ⅔ cup sugar
- ⅔ cup LAND O LAKES® Butter, softened

Filling
- 1 can (21 ounces) cherry fruit filling
- ¾ cup dairy sour cream
- 2 teaspoons almond extract
- ¾ cup sliced toasted almonds

Heat oven to 350°. For crust, in large mixer bowl, combine all crust ingredients. Beat at low speed, scraping bowl often, until mixture is crumbly, 2 to 3 minutes. Press on bottom of ungreased 13×9×2-inch baking pan. Bake for 20 to 25 minutes, or until lightly browned around edges.

For filling, in medium bowl, stir together fruit filling, sour cream and almond extract. Spread over hot crust. Sprinkle nuts over top. Continue baking for 15 to 20 minutes, or until edges are bubbly. Cool completely. Cut into bars. Store, covered, in refrigerator. *Makes about 3 dozen bars*

LAYERED CHOCOLATE BUTTERSCOTCH BARS

The variety of textures and flavors—vanilla wafers, coconut, chocolate, butterscotch and peanuts—is sure-to-please.

- 2½ cups crushed vanilla wafers
- ¼ cup LAND O LAKES® Butter, melted
- 2 teaspoons vanilla
- 1 cup flaked coconut
- 1 cup semi-sweet chocolate chips
- 1 cup butterscotch chips
- 1 can (14 ounces) sweetened condensed milk
- ½ cup salted peanuts

Heat oven to 350°. In small mixer bowl, stir together vanilla wafers, melted butter and vanilla. Press on bottom of greased and floured 13×9×2-inch baking pan. Sprinkle coconut, chocolate chips and butterscotch chips over top. Pour sweetened condensed milk over top; sprinkle with nuts. Bake for 20 to 27 minutes, or until edges are lightly browned. Cool completely. Cut into bars. Store, covered, in refrigerator. *Makes about 3 dozen bars*

Sour Cream Cherry Bars

SWEDISH COCONUT COOKIES

A Scandinavian heritage is the foundation for this buttery, tender cookie.

3½ cups all-purpose flour	1 tablespoon baking powder
2 cups sugar	1 teaspoon baking soda
2 cups LAND O LAKES® Butter, softened	1 teaspoon vanilla
	1 cup flaked coconut

In large mixer bowl, combine flour, sugar, butter, baking powder, baking soda and vanilla. Beat at low speed, scraping bowl often, until well mixed, 3 to 4 minutes. Stir in coconut. Divide dough into halves; shape each half into a 12×2-inch roll. Wrap in waxed paper. Refrigerate until firm, at least 2 hours.

Heat oven to 350°. Cut rolls into ¼-inch slices. Place 2 inches apart on ungreased cookie sheets. Bake for 9 to 14 minutes, or until edges are lightly browned. Cool slightly; remove. *Makes about 8 dozen cookies*

CINNAMON SUGAR CRISPIES

These tender buttery cookies are rolled in cinnamon and sugar for a crisp cookie. A pecan in the center makes them a little more special.

Cookies	¼ teaspoon salt
2 cups all-purpose flour	2 teaspoons vanilla
½ cup sugar	
1 cup LAND O LAKES® Butter, softened	**Sugar Mixture**
1 egg	¼ cup sugar
¼ teaspoon baking soda	½ teaspoon ground cinnamon
	36 pecan halves

Heat oven to 375°. For cookies, in large mixer bowl, combine all cookie ingredients. Beat at low speed, scraping bowl often, until well mixed, 2 to 3 minutes. Shape rounded teaspoonfuls of dough into 1-inch balls.

For sugar mixture, in small bowl, combine sugar and cinnamon. Roll balls in sugar mixture. Place 2 inches apart on greased cookie sheets. Place 1 pecan half in center of each cookie. Bake for 10 to 14 minutes, or until edges are lightly browned. Remove immediately.

Makes about 3 dozen cookies

Swedish Coconut Cookies

TROPICAL ORANGE COCONUT DROPS

Moist coconut and a touch of orange add tropical flavors to these rich butter cookies.

2 cups sugar
1 cup LAND O LAKES® Butter, softened
3 eggs
1 teaspoon baking powder

1 teaspoon salt
1 teaspoon vanilla
1 teaspoon orange extract
3½ cups all-purpose flour
½ cup flaked coconut

Heat oven to 350°. In large mixer bowl, combine sugar, butter, eggs, baking powder, salt, vanilla and orange extract. Beat at low speed, scraping bowl often, until well mixed, 1 to 2 minutes. Stir in flour and coconut until well mixed, 2 to 3 minutes. Drop rounded teaspoonfuls of dough 2 inches apart onto greased cookie sheets. Bake for 8 to 12 minutes, or until edges are lightly browned. Remove immediately. *Makes about 5 dozen cookies*

LEMON DOODLES

Crisp on the outside and chewy on the inside—the lemon flavor adds a new twist to ever popular Snickerdoodles.

2½ cups all-purpose flour
1½ cups sugar
¾ cup flaked coconut
1 cup LAND O LAKES® Butter, softened
2 eggs

1½ teaspoons cream of tartar
1 teaspoon baking soda
¼ teaspoon salt
1 tablespoon lemon juice
½ teaspoon grated lemon peel

Heat oven to 400°. In large mixer bowl, combine all ingredients. Beat at low speed, scraping bowl often, until well mixed, 2 to 4 minutes. Drop rounded teaspoonfuls of dough 2 inches apart onto ungreased cookie sheets. Bake for 7 to 10 minutes, or until edges are lightly browned. Remove immediately. *Makes about 4 dozen cookies*

Tropical Orange Coconut Drops

CHERRY DATE SKILLET COOKIES

Snowy coconut coats these made-in-the-skillet, buttery date cookies.

1 cup LAND O LAKES® Butter
1 cup firmly packed brown
    sugar
1 package (8 ounces) chopped
    dates
1 egg
3 cups crisp rice cereal

1 cup flaked coconut
½ cup chopped maraschino
    cherries, drained
1 tablespoon vanilla
2½ cups flaked coconut for
    rolling

In 10-inch skillet, melt butter over medium heat. Stir in sugar and dates; remove from heat. Stir in egg. Return to heat; continue cooking over medium heat, stirring constantly, until mixture comes to a full boil, 4 to 6 minutes. Boil, stirring constantly, 1 minute; remove from heat. Stir in rice cereal, 1 cup flaked coconut, cherries and vanilla until moistened. Let stand 10 minutes. Shape rounded teaspoonfuls of dough into 1-inch balls. Roll each ball in remaining 2½ cups coconut. *Makes about 5 dozen cookies*

GRANOLA GOODY BARS

These chewy and nutritious snacks are loaded with good-for-you ingredients like granola, raisins, almonds and honey.

2¼ cups granola-type cereal
½ cup all-purpose flour
½ cup sliced almonds
½ cup raisins
¼ cup firmly packed brown
    sugar

½ cup LAND O LAKES® Butter,
    softened
¼ cup honey
½ teaspoon baking soda

Heat oven to 350°. In large mixer bowl, combine all ingredients. Beat at low speed, scraping bowl often, until well mixed, 1 to 2 minutes. Press firmly into ungreased 9-inch square baking pan. Bake for 20 to 25 minutes, or until edges are browned. Cool completely. Cut into bars.
Makes about 2 dozen bars

Cherry Date Skillet Cookies

MOCHA ALMOND BARS

Coffee and almonds give this bar a unique flavor and a crunchy texture.

Bars
2¼ cups all-purpose flour
1 cup granulated sugar
1 cup LAND O LAKES® Butter,
  softened
1 egg
1 teaspoon instant coffee
  granules
1 cup sliced almonds

Glaze
¾ cup powdered sugar
1 to 2 tablespoons milk
¼ teaspoon almond extract

Heat oven to 350°. For bars, in small mixer bowl, combine flour, granulated sugar, butter, egg and instant coffee. Beat at low speed, scraping bowl often, until well mixed, 2 to 3 minutes. Stir in nuts. Press on bottom of greased 13×9×2-inch baking pan. Bake for 25 to 30 minutes, or until edges are lightly browned.

For glaze, in small bowl, stir together all glaze ingredients. Drizzle glaze over warm bars. Cool completely. Cut into bars.

Makes about 3 dozen bars

COCONUT SNOWDROPS

These snowy-white cookies have tender coconut for a moist, chewy cookie.

2 cups all-purpose flour
1 cup flaked coconut
½ cup granulated sugar
1 cup LAND O LAKES® Butter,
  softened

¼ cup milk
1 egg
1 tablespoon vanilla
  Powdered sugar for
  sprinkling

Heat oven to 350°. In large mixer bowl, combine flour, coconut, granulated sugar, butter, milk, egg and vanilla. Beat at low speed, scraping bowl often, until well mixed, 1 to 2 minutes. Drop rounded teaspoonfuls of dough 2 inches apart onto ungreased cookie sheets. Bake for 12 to 15 minutes, or until edges are lightly browned. Remove immediately. Cool completely; sprinkle with powdered sugar.

Makes about 3 dozen cookies

Mocha Almond Bars

GLISTENING CHERRY-FIG BARS

These fruit-filled cake-like bars are sweetly studded with figs and cherries and sprinkled with sugar for a glistening top.

1½ cups all-purpose flour
¾ cup sugar
½ cup LAND O LAKES® Butter, softened
2 eggs
½ teaspoon baking soda

1 teaspoon vanilla
¾ cup chopped figs
¼ cup chopped maraschino cherries, drained
1 tablespoon sugar for sprinkling

Heat oven to 325°. In small mixer bowl, combine flour, ¾ cup sugar, butter, eggs, baking soda and vanilla. Beat at low speed, scraping bowl often, until well mixed, 2 to 3 minutes. Stir in figs and cherries.

Spread into greased and floured 9-inch square baking pan; sprinkle 1 tablespoon sugar over top. Bake for 22 to 30 minutes, or until wooden pick inserted in center comes out clean. Cool completely. Cut into bars.

Makes about 2 dozen bars

SNOWBALL COOKIES

A favorite at Christmas time, pecan-filled Snowball Cookies are scrumptious all year 'round.

2 cups all-purpose flour
2 cups finely chopped pecans
¼ cup granulated sugar
1 cup LAND O LAKES® Butter, softened

1 teaspoon vanilla
Powdered sugar for rolling

Heat oven to 325°. In large mixer bowl, combine flour, nuts, granulated sugar, butter and vanilla. Beat at low speed, scraping bowl often, until well mixed, 3 to 4 minutes. Shape rounded teaspoonfuls of dough into 1-inch balls. Place on ungreased cookie sheets. Bake for 18 to 25 minutes, or until very lightly browned. Remove immediately. Roll in powdered sugar while still warm and again when cool.

Makes about 3 dozen cookies

ALMOND SHORTBREAD BARS

These tender almond bars are perfect with fruit or after dinner coffee.

2 cups all-purpose flour
1 cup sugar
1 cup LAND O LAKES® Butter,
    softened

1 egg, separated
¼ teaspoon almond extract
1 tablespoon water
½ cup chopped almonds

Heat oven to 350°. In large mixer bowl, combine flour, sugar, butter, egg yolk and almond extract. Beat at low speed, scraping bowl often, until particles are fine, 2 to 3 minutes. Press on bottom of greased 15×10×1-inch jelly-roll pan. In small bowl, beat egg white and water until frothy; brush on dough. Sprinkle nuts over top. Bake for 15 to 20 minutes, or until very lightly browned. Cool completely. Cut into bars.   *Makes about 2½ dozen bars*

OLD-WORLD RASPBERRY BARS

This buttery good raspberry-filled bar combines the goodness of Old-World baking and updated convenience.

Crumb Mixture
2¼ cups all-purpose flour
1 cup sugar
1 cup chopped pecans
1 cup LAND O LAKES® Butter,
    softened
1 egg

Filling
1 jar (10 ounces) raspberry
    preserves

Heat oven to 350°. For crumb mixture, in large mixer bowl, combine all crumb ingredients. Beat at low speed, scraping bowl often, until mixture is crumbly, 2 to 3 minutes. Reserve 1½ cups of the crumb mixture. Press remaining crumb mixture on bottom of greased 8-inch square baking pan. Spread preserves to within ½ inch of edges. Crumble 1½ cups reserved crumb mixture over top. Bake for 42 to 50 minutes, or until lightly browned. Cool completely. Cut into bars.   *Makes about 2 dozen bars*

Almond Shortbread Bars

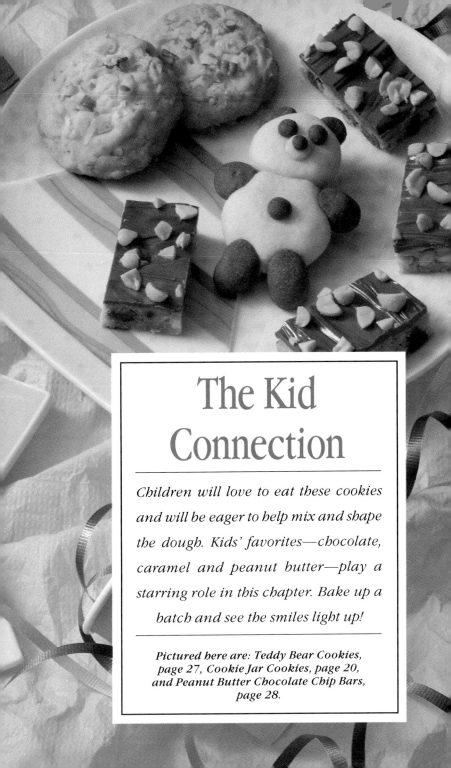

The Kid Connection

Children will love to eat these cookies and will be eager to help mix and shape the dough. Kids' favorites—chocolate, caramel and peanut butter—play a starring role in this chapter. Bake up a batch and see the smiles light up!

Pictured here are: Teddy Bear Cookies, page 27, Cookie Jar Cookies, page 20, and Peanut Butter Chocolate Chip Bars, page 28.

CARAMEL ROCKY ROAD BARS

Crumb Mixture
1 cup all-purpose flour
¾ cup quick-cooking oats
½ cup sugar
½ cup LAND O LAKES® Butter,
  softened
½ teaspoon baking soda
¼ teaspoon salt
¼ cup chopped salted peanuts

Filling
½ cup caramel ice cream
  topping
½ cup salted peanuts
1½ cups miniature
  marshmallows
½ cup milk chocolate chips

Heat oven to 350°. For crumb mixture, in small mixer bowl, combine flour, oats, sugar, butter, baking soda and salt. Beat at low speed, scraping bowl often, until mixture is crumbly, 1 to 2 minutes. Stir in nuts. Reserve ¾ cup of the crumb mixture. Press remaining crumb mixture on bottom of greased and floured 9-inch square baking pan. Bake for 12 to 17 minutes, or until lightly browned.

For filling, spread caramel topping evenly over hot crust. Sprinkle nuts, marshmallows and chocolate chips over top. Crumble ¾ cup reserved crumb mixture over top. Continue baking for 20 to 25 minutes, or until crumb mixture is lightly browned. Cover; refrigerate 1 to 2 hours, or until firm. Cut into bars. *Makes about 2½ dozen bars*

COOKIE JAR COOKIES

Coconut, oats and rice cereal will make these crisp and tender cookies a cookie jar favorite!

3½ cups all-purpose flour
1 cup granulated sugar
1 cup firmly packed brown
  sugar
2 cups LAND O LAKES® Butter,
  softened
1 egg
1 teaspoon cream of tartar

1 teaspoon baking soda
½ teaspoon salt
1 cup quick-cooking oats
1 cup crisp rice cereal
1 cup flaked coconut
½ cup chopped walnuts or
  pecans

Heat oven to 350°. In large mixer bowl, combine flour, granulated sugar, brown sugar, butter, egg, cream of tartar, baking soda and salt. Beat at low speed, scraping bowl often, until well mixed, 2 to 3 minutes. Stir in oats, cereal, coconut and nuts. Drop rounded tablespoonfuls of dough 2 inches apart onto ungreased cookie sheets. Bake for 13 to 16 minutes, or until lightly browned. Remove immediately. *Makes about 4 dozen cookies*

Caramel Rocky Road Bars

BUTTERY JAM TARTS

2½ cups all-purpose flour
½ cup sugar
⅔ cup LAND O LAKES® Butter,
    softened
1 egg
¼ teaspoon baking soda

¼ teaspoon salt
2 tablespoons milk
1 teaspoon almond extract
¾ cup cherry preserves
Sugar for sprinkling

Heat oven to 350°. In large mixer bowl, combine flour, sugar, butter, egg, baking soda, salt, milk and almond extract. Beat at low speed, scraping bowl often, until well mixed, 3 to 4 minutes. Roll out dough, ½ at a time, on well-floured surface, to ⅛-inch thickness. Cut out with 2½-inch round cookie cutter. Place ½ of the cookies 2 inches apart on ungreased cookie sheets. Make small X or a cutout with a very small cookie cutter in top of each remaining cookie. Place level teaspoonfuls of cherry preserves in center of each cookie. Top each with another cookie; press together around edges with fork. Sprinkle with sugar. Bake for 11 to 13 minutes, or until edges are very lightly browned. Remove immediately.

Makes about 2 dozen cookies

TEENTIME DREAM BARS

Crust
1 cup all-purpose flour
⅓ cup sugar
½ cup LAND O LAKES® Butter,
    softened

Filling
½ cup sugar
¼ cup chunky peanut butter
½ cup light corn syrup
2 eggs
¼ teaspoon salt
½ teaspoon vanilla
½ cup flaked coconut
½ cup semi-sweet chocolate
    chips

Heat oven to 350°. For crust, in small mixer bowl, combine all crust ingredients. Beat at low speed, scraping bowl often, until mixture is crumbly, 1 to 2 minutes. Press on bottom of greased 9-inch square baking pan. Bake for 12 to 17 minutes, or until edges are lightly browned.

For filling, in small mixer bowl, combine sugar, peanut butter, corn syrup, eggs, salt and vanilla. Beat at low speed, scraping bowl often, until well mixed, 1 to 2 minutes. Stir in coconut and chocolate chips. Pour over crust. Continue baking for 20 to 30 minutes, or until filling is set and lightly browned. Cool completely. Cut into bars.   *Makes about 3 dozen bars*

Buttery Jam Tarts

TOASTED PECAN TOFFEE BARS

This delicious bar blends the taste and flavor of a cookie and a candy into one special treat.

Bars
- 2 cups all-purpose flour
- 1 cup firmly packed brown sugar
- 1 cup LAND O LAKES® Butter, softened
- 1/2 teaspoon ground cinnamon
- 1 teaspoon vanilla

- 3/4 cup chopped pecans, toasted
- 1/2 cup milk chocolate chips

Topping
- 1/2 cup milk chocolate chips
- 1/4 cup chopped pecans, toasted

Heat oven to 350°. For bars, in large mixer bowl, combine flour, sugar, butter, cinnamon and vanilla. Beat at low speed, scraping bowl often, until mixture is crumbly, 2 to 3 minutes. Stir in nuts and chocolate chips. Press on bottom of greased 13×9×2-inch baking pan. Bake for 25 to 30 minutes, or until edges are lightly browned.

For topping, sprinkle chocolate chips over bars. Let stand 5 minutes to melt. Slightly swirl chips with tip of a knife as they melt, leaving some whole for a marbled effect. *Do not spread chips.* Sprinkle nuts over top. Cool completely. Cut into bars.   *Makes about 3 dozen bars*

OLD-FASHIONED BROWNIES

Brownies, a favorite in every family, are quick, easy and delicious.

- 2 cups all-purpose flour
- 2 cups sugar
- 1/2 cup unsweetened cocoa
- 1 cup LAND O LAKES® Butter, softened

- 2 eggs
- 1 teaspoon vanilla
- 1 cup chopped walnuts or pecans

Heat oven to 350°. In large mixer bowl, combine flour, sugar, cocoa, butter, eggs and vanilla. Beat at low speed, scraping bowl often, until well mixed, 1 to 2 minutes. Stir in nuts. Spread into greased 13×9×2-inch baking pan. Bake for 20 to 25 minutes, or until firm to the touch. Cool completely. Cut into bars.   *Makes about 2 dozen bars*

Toasted Pecan Toffee Bars

BUTTERY CARAMEL CRISPS

12 double graham crackers
2 cups miniature
   marshmallows
¾ cup firmly packed brown
   sugar

¾ cup LAND O LAKES® Butter
1 teaspoon ground cinnamon
1 teaspoon vanilla
1 cup sliced almonds
1 cup flaked coconut

Heat oven to 350°. Line ungreased 15×10×1-inch jelly-roll pan with graham crackers. Sprinkle marshmallows evenly over crackers. In medium saucepan, combine sugar, butter, cinnamon and vanilla. Cook, stirring constantly, over medium heat until sugar is dissolved and butter is melted, 4 to 5 minutes. Pour evenly over crackers and marshmallows; sprinkle nuts and coconut over top. Bake for 8 to 12 minutes, or until lightly browned. Cool completely. Cut into bars.   *Makes about 4 dozen bars*

TEDDY BEAR COOKIES

Cookies become a special treat when shaped into cute little teddy bears.

1 cup sugar
⅔ cup LAND O LAKES® Butter,
   softened
1 egg
2 teaspoons vanilla
2¼ cups all-purpose flour

1 teaspoon baking powder
¼ teaspoon salt
2 squares (1 ounce each)
   unsweetened chocolate,
   melted

Heat oven to 375°. In large mixer bowl, combine sugar, butter, egg and vanilla. Beat at medium speed, scraping bowl often, until well mixed, 1 to 2 minutes. Add flour, baking powder and salt. Continue beating, scraping bowl often, until well mixed, 1 to 2 minutes. Divide dough into halves. Place ½ of the dough in small bowl; blend in melted chocolate.

For each teddy bear, shape a portion of either color dough into a large ball (1-inch) for body, a medium ball (¾-inch) for head, 4 small balls (½-inch) for arms and legs, 2 smaller balls for ears and 1 small ball for nose. If desired, add additional balls for eyes and mouth. Repeat with remaining dough, making either vanilla or chocolate teddy bears or mixing the doughs to make two-tone teddy bears.

To form each cookie, place large ball (body) on ungreased cookie sheet; flatten slightly. Attach head, arms and legs by overlapping slightly onto body. Bake for 7 to 8 minutes, or until body is set. Cool 1 minute on cookie sheet; remove immediately.   *Makes about 2 dozen cookies*

Buttery Caramel Crisps

CHOCOLATE CHUNK COOKIES

Chunks of chocolate and walnuts make these chewy cookies extra special.

¾ cup firmly packed brown
    sugar
½ cup granulated sugar
1 cup LAND O LAKES® Butter,
    softened
1 egg
1½ teaspoons vanilla
2¼ cups all-purpose flour

1 teaspoon baking soda
½ teaspoon salt
1 cup coarsely chopped
    walnuts
1 milk chocolate candy bar
    (8 ounces), cut into ½-inch
    pieces

Heat oven to 375°. In large mixer bowl, combine brown sugar, granulated sugar, butter, egg and vanilla. Beat at medium speed, scraping bowl often, until well mixed, 1 to 2 minutes. Add flour, baking soda and salt. Continue beating until well mixed, 1 to 2 minutes. Stir in nuts and chocolate. Drop rounded tablespoonfuls of dough 2 inches apart onto ungreased cookie sheets. Bake for 9 to 11 minutes, or until lightly browned. Cool 1 minute on cookie sheet; remove immediately. *Makes about 3 dozen cookies*

PEANUT BUTTER CHOCOLATE CHIP BARS

Bars
¾ cup firmly packed brown
    sugar
½ cup granulated sugar
1 cup LAND O LAKES® Butter,
    softened
1 egg
1½ teaspoons vanilla
2¼ cups all-purpose flour
1 teaspoon baking soda

½ teaspoon salt
1 cup chopped peanuts
1 cup semi-sweet chocolate
    chips

Topping
1 cup semi-sweet chocolate
    chips
½ cup creamy peanut butter
½ cup chopped salted peanuts

Heat oven to 375°. For bars, in large mixer bowl, combine brown sugar, granulated sugar, butter, egg and vanilla. Beat at medium speed, scraping bowl often, until well mixed, 1 to 2 minutes. Add flour, baking soda and salt. Continue beating until well mixed, 1 to 2 minutes. Stir in nuts and chips. Press on bottom of ungreased 15×10×1-inch jelly-roll pan. Bake for 12 to 17 minutes, or until edges are lightly browned.

For topping, in small saucepan, combine chocolate chips and peanut butter. Cook over low heat, stirring constantly, until melted, 4 to 5 minutes. Spread over warm bars. Sprinkle nuts over top. Refrigerate until topping sets, about 1 hour. Cut into bars. Store, covered, at room temperature.

Makes about 5 dozen bars

Chocolate Chunk Cookies

CHERRY SCOTCHIES

2 cups all-purpose flour
¾ cup firmly packed brown
    sugar
½ cup flaked coconut
¾ cup LAND O LAKES® Butter,
    softened
1 egg
1 teaspoon baking powder

½ teaspoon salt
2 teaspoons vanilla
½ cup chopped maraschino
    cherries, drained
2 tablespoons all-purpose flour
1 cup butterscotch chips
Powdered sugar for
    sprinkling

Heat oven to 375°. In large mixer bowl, combine 2 cups flour, brown sugar, coconut, butter, egg, baking powder, salt and vanilla. Beat at low speed, scraping bowl often, until well mixed, 1 to 2 minutes. In small bowl, toss together drained maraschino cherries and 2 tablespoons flour. Stir in cherries and butterscotch chips. Spread into greased and floured 13×9×2-inch baking pan. Bake for 20 to 25 minutes, or until edges are lightly browned. Cool completely. Sprinkle with powdered sugar. Cut into bars.

Makes about 3 dozen bars

ROCKY ROAD FUDGE BROWNIES

Bars
½ cup LAND O LAKES® Butter
2 squares (1 ounce each)
    unsweetened chocolate
2 eggs
1 cup sugar
⅔ cup all-purpose flour
¼ teaspoon salt
1 teaspoon vanilla

Topping
½ cup chopped salted peanuts
½ cup butterscotch chips
1 cup miniature marshmallows
¼ cup chocolate ice cream
    topping

Heat oven to 350°. For bars, in heavy, small saucepan, combine butter and chocolate. Cook, stirring constantly, over medium heat, until melted, 3 to 5 minutes; set aside.

In small mixer bowl, beat eggs at medium speed until light and fluffy, 2 to 3 minutes. Gradually beat in cooled chocolate mixture, sugar, flour, salt and vanilla, scraping bowl often, until well mixed, 1 to 2 minutes. Spread into greased 9-inch square baking pan. Bake for 20 to 25 minutes, or until brownies begin to pull away from sides of pan.

For topping, sprinkle nuts, butterscotch chips and marshmallows over hot brownies. Drizzle with ice-cream topping. Continue baking for 12 to 18 minutes, or until lightly browned. Cool completely. Cut into bars.

Makes about 2 dozen bars

Cherry Scotchies

Irresistible Bars

This chapter has bars for everyone—buttery-rich shortbread, fruit, chocolate, nut and cheesecake. Most of these are so easy, you just mix, pat-in-the-pan and bake; then finish with glazes or wonderful-tasting fillings and toppings. Try them—they're sure to be a hit with your family and friends.

Pictured here are: Crisp 'n' Crunchy Almond Coconut Bars, page 34, and Strawberry Wonders, page 37.

CHERRY DATE SPARKLE BARS

Crust
- 1 cup all-purpose flour
- ¼ cup sugar
- ½ cup LAND O LAKES® Butter, softened

Filling
- ¾ cup sugar
- ½ cup all-purpose flour
- 2 eggs
- ½ teaspoon baking powder
- ¼ teaspoon salt
- 1½ teaspoons vanilla
- ¾ cup chopped dates
- ½ cup flaked coconut
- ½ cup chopped pecans
- ½ cup halved maraschino cherries, drained

Heat oven to 350°. For crust, in small mixer bowl, combine all crust ingredients. Beat at low speed, scraping bowl often, until mixture is crumbly, 1 to 2 minutes. Press on bottom of ungreased 9-inch square baking pan. Bake for 15 to 20 minutes, or until edges are lightly browned.

For filling, in same mixer bowl, combine sugar, flour, eggs, baking powder, salt and vanilla. Beat at medium speed, scraping bowl often, until well mixed, 1 to 2 minutes. Stir in remaining ingredients. Pour over hot crust. Continue baking for 25 to 30 minutes, or until lightly browned and filling is set. Cool completely. Cut into bars.   *Makes about 3 dozen bars*

CRISP 'N' CRUNCHY ALMOND COCONUT BARS

Crust
- 1¼ cups all-purpose flour
- ¼ cup granulated sugar
- ½ cup LAND O LAKES® Butter, softened
- ½ teaspoon rum extract
- ¼ cup sliced almonds, toasted

Filling
- 1 cup powdered sugar
- ¼ cup LAND O LAKES® Butter
- ¼ cup milk
- 2 tablespoons all-purpose flour
- ½ teaspoon rum extract
- 1 cup flaked coconut
- 1 cup sliced almonds

Heat oven to 375°. For crust, in small mixer bowl, combine flour, granulated sugar, butter and rum extract. Beat at low speed, scraping bowl often, until mixture is crumbly, 1 to 2 minutes. Stir in nuts. Press on bottom of ungreased 9-inch square baking pan. Bake for 12 to 18 minutes, or until edges are lightly browned.

For filling, in small saucepan, combine powdered sugar, butter, milk, flour and rum extract. Cook, stirring constantly, over medium heat until mixture comes to a full boil, 5 to 7 minutes. Stir in coconut and nuts. Pour over crust. Continue baking for 11 to 16 minutes, or until lightly browned. Cool completely. Cut into bars.   *Makes about 2 dozen bars*

Cherry Date Sparkle Bars

TWIST O'LEMON CHEESECAKES

Crust
2 cups all-purpose flour
½ cup sugar
¾ cup LAND O LAKES® Butter,
  softened
1 tablespoon grated lemon peel

Filling
1⅓ cups sugar
¼ cup all-purpose flour
2 packages (3 ounces each)
  cream cheese, softened
4 eggs
¼ cup lemon juice
1 teaspoon baking powder
½ teaspoon salt
1 tablespoon grated lemon peel
1 teaspoon vanilla
1 cup sliced almonds
1 teaspoon ground nutmeg

Heat oven to 350°. For crust, in large mixer bowl, combine all crust ingredients. Beat at low speed, scraping bowl often, until particles are fine, 1 to 2 minutes. Press on bottom of ungreased 13×9×2-inch baking pan. Bake for 15 to 20 minutes, or until edges are lightly browned.

For filling, in same mixer bowl, combine all filling ingredients except nuts and nutmeg. Beat at low speed, scraping bowl often, until well mixed. Stir in nuts. Pour over hot crust. Continue baking for 20 to 25 minutes, or until knife inserted in center comes out clean. Sprinkle nutmeg over top. Cool. Store, covered, in refrigerator. *Makes about 3 dozen bars*

STRAWBERRY WONDERS

Crust
1½ cups all-purpose flour
½ cup quick-cooking oats
½ cup granulated sugar
¾ cup LAND O LAKES® Butter,
  softened
½ teaspoon baking soda

Topping
¾ cup flaked coconut
¾ cup chopped walnuts
¼ cup all-purpose flour
¼ cup packed brown sugar
2 tablespoons LAND O LAKES®
  Butter, softened
½ teaspoon ground cinnamon
1 jar (10 ounces) strawberry
  preserves

Heat oven to 350°. For crust, in large mixer bowl, combine all crust ingredients. Beat at low speed, scraping bowl often, until mixture is crumbly, 1 to 2 minutes. Press crust mixture on bottom of greased 13×9×2-inch baking pan. Bake for 18 to 22 minutes, or until edges are lightly browned.

For topping, in same mixer bowl, combine coconut, nuts, flour, brown sugar, butter and cinnamon. Beat at low speed, scraping bowl often, until well mixed. Spread preserves to ¼ inch of edges of hot crust. Sprinkle topping mixture over preserves. Continue baking for 18 to 22 minutes, or until edges are lightly browned. Cool. *Makes about 3 dozen bars*

Twist O'Lemon Cheesecakes

APPLE PIE BARS

Apple pie takes on a new look in these rich apple bars that are topped with a vanilla glaze.

Crust
Milk
1 egg yolk, reserve egg white
2½ cups all-purpose flour
1 teaspoon salt
1 cup LAND O LAKES® Butter, softened

Filling
1 cup crushed corn flake cereal
8 cups peeled, cored, ¼-inch sliced, tart cooking apples (about 8 to 10 medium)
1 cup granulated sugar
1½ teaspoons ground cinnamon
½ teaspoon ground nutmeg
1 reserved egg white
2 tablespoons granulated sugar
½ teaspoon ground cinnamon

Glaze
1 cup powdered sugar
1 to 2 tablespoons milk
½ teaspoon vanilla

Heat oven to 350°. For crust, add enough milk to egg yolk to measure ⅔ cup; set aside. In medium bowl, combine flour and salt. Cut in butter until crumbly. With fork, stir in milk mixture until dough forms a ball; divide into halves. Roll out ½ of the dough, on lightly floured surface, into a 15×10-inch rectangle. Place on bottom of ungreased 15×10×1-inch jelly-roll pan.

For filling, sprinkle cereal over top; layer apples over cereal. In small bowl, combine 1 cup granulated sugar, 1½ teaspoons cinnamon and nutmeg. Sprinkle over apples. Roll remaining ½ of dough into a 15½×10½-inch rectangle; place over apples. In small bowl, with fork beat egg white until foamy; brush over top crust. In another small bowl, stir together 2 tablespoons granulated sugar and ½ teaspoon cinnamon; sprinkle over crust. Bake for 45 to 60 minutes, or until lightly browned.

For glaze, in small bowl, stir together all glaze ingredients. Drizzle over warm bars. Cut into bars.   *Makes about 3 dozen bars*

Apple Pie Bars

CARAMEL CHOCOLATE PECAN BARS

Crust
- 2 cups all-purpose flour
- 1 cup firmly packed brown sugar
- ½ cup LAND O LAKES® Butter, softened
- 1 cup pecan halves

Filling
- ½ cup firmly packed brown sugar
- ⅔ cup LAND O LAKES® Butter
- ½ cup semi-sweet chocolate chips
- ½ cup butterscotch chips

Heat oven to 350°. For crust, in large mixer bowl, combine flour, sugar and butter. Beat at medium speed, scraping bowl often, until particles are fine, 2 to 3 minutes. Press on bottom of ungreased 13×9×2-inch baking pan. Sprinkle nuts over crust.

For filling, in small saucepan, combine sugar and butter. Cook, stirring constantly, over medium heat until mixture comes to a full boil, 4 to 5 minutes. Boil, stirring constantly, until candy thermometer reaches 242°F, or small amount of mixture dropped into ice water forms a firm ball, about 1 minute. Pour over pecans and crust.

Bake for 18 to 20 minutes, or until entire caramel layer is bubbly. Immediately sprinkle with chocolate and butterscotch chips. Let stand 3 to 5 minutes to melt chips. Swirl chips with tip of knife, leaving some whole for a marbled effect. Cool. Cut into bars. *Makes about 3 dozen bars*

COCONUT DATE CANDY SQUARES

Bars
- 1 cup chopped dates
- ¾ cup granulated sugar
- ½ cup all-purpose flour
- ½ cup LAND O LAKES® Butter
- 1 egg
- 1½ cups flaked coconut

Glaze
- ¼ cup powdered sugar
- 2 teaspoons milk
- ½ teaspoon lemon juice
- ¼ teaspoon vanilla

For bars, in heavy, medium saucepan, combine dates, granulated sugar, flour, butter and egg. Cook, stirring constantly, over medium heat until mixture comes to a full boil, 7 to 9 minutes. Continue cooking, stirring constantly, until thickened, 3 minutes. Stir in coconut. Spread in greased 9×5×3-inch loaf pan.

For glaze, in small bowl, stir together all glaze ingredients. Drizzle glaze over warm bars. Cover; refrigerate until firm, about 3 hours. Cut into squares. Store, covered, in refrigerator. *Makes about 2 dozen squares*

Caramel Chocolate Pecan Bars

ALMOND MACAROON BARS

This rich macaroon bar is glorified with coconut and almonds.

Crust
1¾ cups all-purpose flour
½ cup sugar
¾ cup LAND O LAKES® Butter,
    softened
½ teaspoon ground nutmeg

Filling
1 cup sugar
2 eggs
2 tablespoons all-purpose flour
1 teaspoon baking powder
½ teaspoon salt
2 teaspoons vanilla
1 cup flaked coconut
1 cup toasted slivered almonds

Heat oven to 350°. For crust, in small mixer bowl, combine all crust ingredients. Beat at low speed, scraping bowl often, until particles are fine, 2 to 3 minutes. Press on bottom of ungreased 13×9×2-inch baking pan. Bake for 15 to 20 minutes, or until edges are lightly browned.

For filling, in same mixer bowl, combine sugar, eggs, flour, baking powder, salt and vanilla. Beat at medium speed, scraping bowl often, until well mixed, 1 to 2 minutes. Stir in coconut and nuts. Pour over hot crust. Continue baking for 15 to 20 minutes.   *Makes about 3 dozen bars*

PINEAPPLE CHEESECAKE BARS

Crumb Mixture
1¼ cups all-purpose flour
⅓ cup sugar
½ cup LAND O LAKES® Butter
1 tablespoon grated orange
    peel

Filling
1 package (8 ounces) cream
    cheese, softened
¼ cup sugar
1 egg
1 tablespoon lemon juice
½ cup chopped candied
    pineapple

Heat oven to 350°. For crumb mixture, in small mixer bowl, combine all crumb mixture ingredients. Beat at low speed, scraping bowl often, until well mixed, 1 to 2 minutes. Reserve ½ cup of the crumb mixture. Press remaining crumb mixture on bottom of ungreased 8-inch square baking pan. Bake for 12 to 17 minutes, or until edges are lightly browned.

For filling, in same mixer bowl, combine cream cheese, sugar, egg and lemon juice. Beat at medium speed, scraping bowl often, until mixture is light and fluffy, 1 to 2 minutes. Stir in pineapple. Spread filling over hot crust. Sprinkle ½ cup reserved crumb mixture over top. Continue baking for 15 to 20 minutes, or until edges are lightly browned. Cool completely. Cut into bars. Store, covered, in refrigerator.   *Makes about 2 dozen bars*

Almond Macaroon Bars

FROSTED HONEY BARS

Bars
1½ cups all-purpose flour
1 cup LAND O LAKES® Butter, melted
1 cup honey
3 eggs
1½ teaspoons baking soda
1 teaspoon ground cinnamon
¾ teaspoon salt
1½ cups shredded carrots (about 3 medium)
¾ cup chopped walnuts

Frosting
1 cup powdered sugar
1 package (8 ounces) cream cheese, softened
1 teaspoon milk
1 teaspoon vanilla

Heat oven to 350°. For bars, in large mixer bowl, combine flour, butter, honey, eggs, baking soda, cinnamon and salt. Beat at low speed, scraping bowl often, until well mixed, 1 to 2 minutes. Stir in carrots and nuts. Pour into greased 15×10×1-inch jelly-roll pan. Bake for 20 to 25 minutes, or until top springs back when touched lightly in center. Cool completely.

For frosting, in small mixer bowl, combine all frosting ingredients. Beat at medium speed, scraping bowl often, until smooth, 1 to 2 minutes. Frost; cut into bars. Store, covered, in refrigerator.   *Makes about 3 dozen bars*

SUNNY LEMON OATMEAL BARS

The ultimate in tenderness is found inside this lemon oatmeal bar.

Bars
1¼ cups all-purpose flour
¾ cup quick-cooking oats
⅔ cup granulated sugar
1 cup LAND O LAKES® Butter, softened
½ cup milk
1 egg
1 teaspoon baking soda
½ teaspoon salt
1 tablespoon grated lemon peel
1 teaspoon vanilla

Glaze
1 cup powdered sugar
2 tablespoons lemon juice
1 tablespoon grated lemon peel

Heat oven to 375°. For bars, in large mixer bowl, combine all bar ingredients. Beat at low speed, scraping bowl often, until well mixed, 1 to 2 minutes. Spread into ungreased 13×9×2-inch baking pan. Bake for 15 to 20 minutes, or until wooden pick inserted in center comes out clean.

For glaze, in small bowl, combine all glaze ingredients; stir until smooth. Spread over warm bars. Cool.   *Makes about 3 dozen bars*

Frosted Honey Bars

JAN HAGEL

This traditional Scandinavian bar just melts in your mouth.

---

2 cups all-purpose flour
1 cup sugar
1 cup LAND O LAKES® Butter,
   softened

1 egg, separated
1 teaspoon ground cinnamon
½ teaspoon salt
1 cup sliced almonds

Heat oven to 350°. In large mixer bowl, combine flour, sugar, butter, egg yolk, cinnamon and salt. Beat at low speed, scraping bowl often, until well mixed, 2 to 3 minutes. Divide dough into halves. Press each half onto an ungreased cookie sheet to 1/16-inch thickness. In small bowl, beat egg white with fork until foamy. Brush over dough; sprinkle with nuts. Bake for 12 to 15 minutes, or until very lightly browned. Immediately cut into 2-inch squares and remove from pan. Cool completely.

Makes 3 to 4 dozen squares

ORANGE DATE TREASURE BARS

Help yourself to this luxuriously moist, old-fashioned date bar.

Bars
  1 package (8 ounces) chopped
    dates
  ¾ cup granulated sugar
  ½ cup LAND O LAKES® Butter
  ½ cup water
  1¼ cups all-purpose flour
  1 cup chopped pecans
  ¾ cup milk
  ¼ cup orange juice
  2 eggs
  ¾ teaspoon baking soda

¼ teaspoon salt
1 tablespoon grated orange
  peel

Frosting
  3 cups powdered sugar
  ⅓ cup LAND O LAKES® Butter,
    softened
  3 tablespoons milk
  1 tablespoon grated orange
    peel

Heat oven to 350°. For bars, in large saucepan, combine dates, granulated sugar, butter and water. Cook, stirring constantly, over low heat, until dates are softened, 5 to 8 minutes. Remove from heat; stir in flour, nuts, milk, orange juice, eggs, baking soda, salt and orange peel. Spread onto greased 15×10×1-inch jelly-roll pan. Bake for 15 to 20 minutes, or until wooden pick inserted in center comes out clean. Cool completely.

For frosting, in small bowl, combine all frosting ingredients. Beat at medium speed, scraping bowl often, until light and fluffy, 1 to 2 minutes. Spread over bars. Cut into bars.

Makes about 4 dozen bars

Jan Hagel

CITRUS PIE BARS

These moist pie-like bars have just the right touch of tropical flavor.

Crust
- 1 cup all-purpose flour
- ¼ cup sugar
- ⅓ cup LAND O LAKES® Butter, softened
- ¼ teaspoon ground cardamom or mace

Filling
- ½ cup sugar
- ½ cup flaked coconut
- 2 eggs
- 2 tablespoons all-purpose flour
- ½ teaspoon baking powder
- ⅛ teaspoon salt
- 2 tablespoons grated lemon or orange peel
- 2 tablespoons lemon juice

Heat oven to 350°. For crust, in small mixer bowl, combine all crust ingredients. Beat at low speed, scraping bowl often, until particles are fine, 1 to 2 minutes. Press on bottom of ungreased 8-inch square baking pan. Bake for 12 to 17 minutes, or until edges are lightly browned.

For filling, in same mixer bowl, combine all filling ingredients. Beat at medium speed, scraping bowl often, until well mixed, 1 to 2 minutes. Pour over hot crust. Continue baking for 15 to 20 minutes, or until edges are lightly brown. Cool completely. Cut into bars.

Makes about 2 dozen bars

SPICE 'N' EASY APPLE RAISIN BARS

These buttery good homemade bars are quick to make and full of flavor.

Crumb Mixture
- 2 cups all-purpose flour
- 2 cups quick-cooking oats
- 1½ cups sugar
- 1¼ cups LAND O LAKES® Butter, melted
- 1 teaspoon baking soda

Filling
- ½ cup raisins
- ½ cup chopped pecans
- 1 can (20 ounces) apple fruit filling
- ½ teaspoon ground cinnamon
- ½ teaspoon ground nutmeg

Heat oven to 350°. For crumb mixture, in large bowl, combine all crumb ingredients. Stir until well mixed, 1 to 2 minutes. Reserve 1½ cups of the crumb mixture. Press remaining crumb mixture on bottom of ungreased 13×9×2-inch baking pan. Bake for 15 to 20 minutes, or until edges are lightly browned.

For filling, in same bowl, combine all filling ingredients. Stir to blend. Spread over hot crust. Sprinkle 1½ cups reserved crumb mixture over top. Continue baking for 25 to 30 minutes, or until lightly browned. Cool completely. Cut into bars.

Makes about 3 dozen bars

Citrus Pie Bars

GLAZED RUM RAISIN BARS

Bars
- ½ cup water
- 1 cup raisins
- 2 cups all-purpose flour
- ¾ cup granulated sugar
- 1 cup LAND O LAKES® Butter, softened
- ½ cup milk
- 1 egg
- 1 teaspoon baking powder
- 1 teaspoon salt
- ½ teaspoon rum extract

Glaze
- ¼ cup LAND O LAKES® Butter
- ¾ cup powdered sugar
- 1 tablespoon water
- ¼ teaspoon rum extract

Heat oven to 375°. For bars, in heavy, small saucepan, combine water and raisins. Cook over medium heat until water comes to a full boil, 3 to 4 minutes. Drain water; reserve raisins.

In large mixer bowl, combine flour, granulated sugar, butter, milk, egg, baking powder, salt and rum extract. Beat at low speed, scraping bowl often, until well mixed, 2 to 3 minutes. Stir in drained raisins. Spread into ungreased 13×9×2-inch baking pan. Bake for 20 to 25 minutes, or until wooden pick inserted in center comes out clean.

For glaze, in same saucepan, melt butter over low heat, 3 to 4 minutes. Add powdered sugar, water and rum extract. Cook, stirring occasionally, until smooth, 1 to 2 minutes. Spread glaze over warm bars. Cool completely. Cut into bars. *Makes about 3 dozen bars*

HONEY NUT CHESS BARS

Crust
- 1¼ cups all-purpose flour
- ⅓ cup granulated sugar
- ½ cup LAND O LAKES® Butter, softened
- ¼ cup chopped pecans

Filling
- 1 cup firmly packed brown sugar
- ½ cup chopped pecans
- ½ cup LAND O LAKES® Butter, melted
- 2 eggs
- 2 tablespoons honey

Heat oven to 350°. For crust, in small mixer bowl, combine flour, sugar and butter. Beat at low speed, scraping bowl often, until mixture is crumbly, 1 to 2 minutes. Stir in nuts. Press on bottom of ungreased 9-inch square baking pan. Bake for 15 to 20 minutes, or until edges are lightly browned.

For filling, in same mixer bowl, combine all filling ingredients. Beat at low speed, scraping bowl often, until well mixed, 1 to 2 minutes. Pour over hot crust. Continue baking for 25 to 30 minutes, or until wooden pick inserted in center comes out clean. Cool. *Makes about 3 dozen bars*

Glazed Rum Raisin Bars; Pineapple Cheesecake Bars, page 42

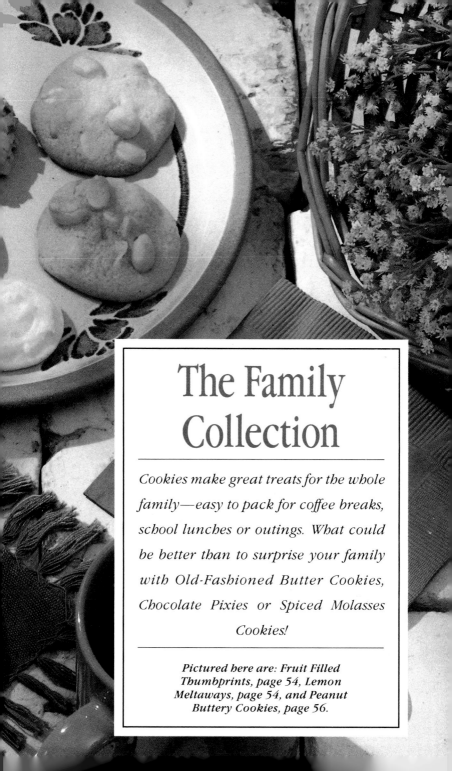

The Family Collection

Cookies make great treats for the whole family—easy to pack for coffee breaks, school lunches or outings. What could be better than to surprise your family with Old-Fashioned Butter Cookies, Chocolate Pixies or Spiced Molasses Cookies!

Pictured here are: Fruit Filled Thumbprints, page 54, Lemon Meltaways, page 54, and Peanut Buttery Cookies, page 56.

LEMON MELTAWAYS

These tiny refrigerator cookies are lemon flavored with lemon frosting.

Cookies
1¼ cups all-purpose flour
½ cup cornstarch
⅓ cup powdered sugar
¾ cup LAND O LAKES® Butter,
    softened
1 tablespoon lemon juice
1 teaspoon lemon peel

Frosting
¾ cup powdered sugar
¼ cup LAND O LAKES® Butter,
    softened
1 teaspoon lemon juice
1 teaspoon grated lemon peel

For cookies, in large mixer bowl, combine all cookie ingredients. Beat at low speed, scraping bowl often, until well mixed, 2 to 3 minutes. Shape dough into two 8×1-inch rolls. Wrap in waxed paper. Refrigerate until firm, 1 to 2 hours.

Heat oven to 350°. Cut rolls into ¼-inch slices. Place 2 inches apart on ungreased cookie sheets. Bake for 8 to 12 minutes, or until set; cookies will not brown. Remove immediately; cool completely.

For frosting, in small mixer bowl, combine all frosting ingredients. Beat at medium speed, scraping bowl often, until light and fluffy, 1 to 2 minutes. Spread on cooled cookies. *Makes about 4 dozen cookies*

FRUIT FILLED THUMBPRINTS

These tender butter cookies are rolled in nuts and filled with fruit preserves.

2 cups all-purpose flour
½ cup firmly packed brown
    sugar
1 cup LAND O LAKES® Butter,
    softened

2 eggs, separated
⅛ teaspoon salt
1 teaspoon vanilla
1½ cups finely chopped pecans
    Fruit preserves

Heat oven to 350°. In large mixer bowl, combine flour, sugar, butter, egg yolks, salt and vanilla. Beat at low speed, scraping bowl often, until well mixed, 2 to 3 minutes. Shape rounded teaspoonfuls of dough into 1-inch balls. In small bowl, beat egg whites with fork until foamy. Dip each ball into whites; roll in nuts. Place 1 inch apart on greased cookie sheets. Make a depression in center of each cookie with back of teaspoon. Bake for 8 minutes; remove from oven. Fill centers with preserves. Continue baking for 6 to 10 minutes, or until lightly browned.

Makes about 3 dozen cookies

OLD-FASHIONED BUTTER COOKIES

Passed down for four generations, this buttery sugar cookie recipe brings back fond memories of Grandma's cookie jar.

---

³⁄₄ cup sugar
1 cup LAND O LAKES® Butter,
   softened
2 egg yolks

1 teaspoon vanilla
2 cups all-purpose flour
¹⁄₄ teaspoon salt
Pecan halves

Heat oven to 350°. In large mixer bowl, combine sugar, butter, egg yolks and vanilla. Beat at medium speed, scraping bowl often, until well mixed, 1 to 2 minutes. Add flour and salt; beat at low speed, scraping bowl often, until well mixed, 2 to 3 minutes. Shape rounded teaspoonfuls of dough into 1-inch balls. Place 2 inches apart on ungreased cookie sheets. Flatten cookie to ¹⁄₄-inch thickness with bottom of glass dipped in sugar. Place pecan half in center of each cookie. Bake for 10 to 12 minutes, or until edges are lightly browned. Cool 1 minute; remove from cookie sheets.

Makes about 2¹⁄₂ dozen cookies

COUNTRY SOUR CREAM COOKIES

Passed on to three generations of moms, these cutout cookies are a holiday favorite.

---

4 cups all-purpose flour
2 cups sugar
1 cup LAND O LAKES® Butter,
   softened
¹⁄₂ cup dairy sour cream
2 eggs
1 tablespoon baking powder

1 teaspoon baking soda
¹⁄₂ teaspoon salt
¹⁄₂ teaspoon ground nutmeg
1 teaspoon vanilla
¹⁄₂ teaspoon lemon extract
Sugar for sprinkling

In large mixer bowl, combine 2 cups of the flour, 2 cups sugar, butter, sour cream, eggs, baking powder, baking soda, salt, nutmeg, vanilla and lemon extract. Beat at low speed, scraping bowl often, until well mixed, 2 to 3 minutes. Stir in remaining 2 cups flour. Divide dough into 4 equal portions. Wrap in waxed paper. Refrigerate until firm, at least 2 hours.

Heat oven to 350°. Roll out dough on well-floured surface to ¹⁄₈-inch thickness. Cut out with cookie cutters. Place 1 inch apart on ungreased cookie sheets. Sprinkle sugar over tops. Bake for 8 to 12 minutes, or until edges are lightly browned.

Makes about 6 dozen cookies

Note: Dough may be tinted with a few drops of food coloring before it is refrigerated.

BANANA CREAM SANDWICH COOKIES

*These banana cookies are fun to make and are filled with a buttery
frosting for a delicious sandwich cookie.*

Cookies
2¹/₃ cups all-purpose flour
1 cup granulated sugar
1 cup LAND O LAKES® Butter,
    softened
¹/₂ cup banana cut into ¹/₄-inch
    slices (about 1 medium)
¹/₄ teaspoon salt
1 teaspoon vanilla
¹/₂ cup chopped pecans

Frosting
3 cups powdered sugar
¹/₃ cup LAND O LAKES® Butter,
    softened
3 to 4 tablespoons milk
1 teaspoon vanilla
    Food coloring (optional)

Heat oven to 350°. For cookies, in large mixer bowl, combine flour, granulated sugar, butter, banana, salt and vanilla. Beat at low speed, scraping bowl often, until well mixed, 2 to 3 minutes. Stir in nuts. Shape rounded teaspoonfuls of dough into 1-inch balls. Place 2 inches apart on greased cookie sheets. Flatten cookies to ¹/₄-inch thickness with bottom of glass dipped in flour. Bake for 12 to 15 minutes, or until edges are lightly browned. Remove immediately; cool completely.

For frosting, in small mixer bowl, combine all frosting ingredients. Beat at medium speed, scraping bowl often, until light and fluffy, 1 to 2 minutes. If desired, tint with food coloring. Spread 1 tablespoon of frosting over bottoms of ¹/₂ of the cookies. Top with remaining cookies.

Makes about 2 dozen sandwich cookies

PEANUT BUTTERY COOKIES

1¹/₂ cups all-purpose flour
¹/₂ cup granulated sugar
¹/₂ cup firmly packed brown
    sugar
¹/₂ cup LAND O LAKES® Butter,
    softened

2 eggs
1 teaspoon salt
¹/₂ teaspoon baking soda
¹/₂ teaspoon vanilla
2 cups salted peanuts (about
    12 ounces)

Heat oven to 350°. In large mixer bowl, combine flour, granulated sugar, brown sugar, butter, eggs, salt, baking soda and vanilla. Beat at low speed, scraping bowl often, until well mixed, 2 to 3 minutes. Stir in nuts. Drop rounded teaspoonfuls of dough 2 inches apart onto greased cookie sheets. Bake for 8 to 12 minutes, or until lightly browned. Remove immediately.

Makes about 4 dozen cookies

Banana Cream Sandwich Cookies

FAVORITE BUTTER COOKIES

These crisp, tender cutout cookies can be decorated to capture the spirit of your occasion.

Cookies
2½ cups all-purpose flour
1 cup granulated sugar
1 cup LAND O LAKES® Butter,
  softened
1 egg
1 teaspoon baking powder
2 tablespoons orange juice
1 tablespoon vanilla

Frosting
4 cups powdered sugar
½ cup LAND O LAKES® Butter,
  softened
3 to 4 tablespoons milk
2 teaspoons vanilla
Food coloring, colored
  sugars, flaked coconut and
  cinnamon candies for
  decorations

For cookies, in large mixer bowl, combine all cookie ingredients. Beat at low speed, scraping bowl often, until well mixed, 1 to 2 minutes. If desired, divide dough into 3 equal portions; color ⅔ of the dough with desired food colorings. Mix until dough is evenly colored. Wrap in waxed paper. Refrigerate until firm, 2 to 3 hours.

Heat oven to 400°. Roll out dough, ⅓ at a time, on well-floured surface to ¼-inch thickness. Cut out with 3-inch cookie cutters. Place 1 inch apart on ungreased cookie sheets. If desired, sprinkle colored sugars over tops, or bake and decorate later. Bake for 6 to 10 minutes, or until edges are lightly browned. Remove immediately; cool completely.

For frosting, in small mixer bowl, combine powdered sugar, butter, milk and vanilla. Beat at low speed, scraping bowl often, until fluffy, 1 to 2 minutes. Frost or decorate cooled cookies.   *Makes about 3 dozen cookies*

Decorating ideas:
Wreaths: Cut out cookies with 2-inch round cookie cutter; bake as directed. Frost with green colored frosting. Color coconut green; sprinkle frosted cookies with coconut. Place 3 cinnamon candies together to resemble holly.

Christmas trees: Color dough green; cut out with Christmas tree cutter. Sprinkle with colored sugars; bake as directed.

Angels: Cut out cookies with angel cookie cutter; bake as directed. Use blue frosting for dress, yellow frosting for hair and white frosting for wings, face and lace on dress.

Favorite Butter Cookies

CANDY AND PEANUT JUMBLES

You'll receive lots of requests for these colorful cookies.

1 cup granulated sugar
1 cup firmly packed brown
    sugar
1 cup LAND O LAKES® Butter,
    softened
2 eggs
1 tablespoon vanilla
2 cups all-purpose flour

1½ cups quick-cooking oats
1 teaspoon baking soda
½ teaspoon salt
2 cups (1 pound) candy coated
    milk chocolate pieces
1 cup coarsely chopped salted
    peanuts

Heat oven to 350°. In large mixer bowl, combine granulated sugar, brown sugar, butter, eggs and vanilla. Beat at medium speed, scraping bowl often, until light and fluffy, 2 to 3 minutes. Add flour, oats, baking soda and salt. Beat at medium speed, scraping bowl often, until well mixed, 2 to 3 minutes. Stir in candy and nuts. Drop scant ¼ cupfuls of dough 2 inches apart onto greased cookie sheets. Bake for 14 to 18 minutes, or until golden brown. Remove immediately. *Makes about 2 dozen cookies*

HONEY 'N' SPICE COOKIES

Orange, honey, nutmeg and cloves team up in these buttery tender, soft drop cookies.

Cookies
2 cups all-purpose flour
¾ cup granulated sugar
¾ cup LAND O LAKES® Butter,
    softened
¼ cup honey
1 egg
½ teaspoon salt
½ teaspoon baking soda

½ teaspoon ground nutmeg
¼ teaspoon ground cloves
½ teaspoon orange extract or
    vanilla

Glaze
1 cup powdered sugar
2 tablespoons milk
2 teaspoons grated orange peel

Heat oven to 375°. For cookies, in large mixer bowl, combine all cookie ingredients. Beat at low speed, scraping bowl often, until well mixed, 1 to 2 minutes. Drop rounded teaspoonfuls of dough 2 inches apart onto ungreased cookie sheets. Bake for 7 to 10 minutes, or until edges are lightly browned. Remove immediately.

For glaze, in small bowl, stir together all glaze ingredients. Frost warm cookies with glaze. *Makes about 3 dozen cookies*

Candy and Peanut Jumbles

MAPLE RAISIN COOKIES

Cookies
2¼ cups all-purpose flour
1 cup granulated sugar
¾ cup LAND O LAKES® Butter, softened
¾ cup applesauce
1 egg
1 teaspoon pumpkin pie spice
½ teaspoon baking soda
½ teaspoon salt

1 cup raisins
½ cup chopped walnuts

Frosting
4 cups powdered sugar
½ cup LAND O LAKES® Butter, softened
3 to 4 tablespoons milk
½ teaspoon maple extract
Raisins

Heat oven to 375°. For cookies, in large mixer bowl, combine flour, granulated sugar, butter, applesauce, egg, pumpkin pie spice, baking soda and salt. Beat at low speed, scraping bowl often, until well mixed, 2 to 3 minutes. Stir in raisins and nuts. Drop rounded teaspoonfuls of dough 2 inches apart onto greased cookie sheets. Bake for 10 to 12 minutes, or until lightly browned. Remove immediately; cool completely.

For frosting, in small mixer bowl, combine powdered sugar, butter, milk and maple extract. Beat at medium speed, scraping bowl often, until light and fluffy, 3 to 4 minutes. Spread over cooled cookies. Place 2 raisins in center of each cookie.   *Makes about 3 dozen cookies*

CORNISH BISCUIT COOKIES

These soft cookies, filled with raisins, have been a traditional family recipe for over 100 years.

3½ cups all-purpose flour
¾ cup firmly packed brown sugar
½ cup granulated sugar
1 cup LAND O LAKES® Butter, softened
1 cup milk
2 eggs

2 teaspoons baking powder
½ teaspoon baking soda
½ teaspoon salt
2 teaspoons vanilla
1 cup raisins
Granulated sugar for sprinkling

Heat oven to 375°. In large mixer bowl, combine flour, brown sugar, granulated sugar, butter, milk, eggs, baking powder, baking soda, salt and vanilla. Beat at low speed, scraping bowl often, until well mixed, 2 to 3 minutes. Stir in raisins. Drop rounded teaspoonfuls of dough 2 inches apart onto greased cookie sheets. Sprinkle sugar over tops. Bake for 8 to 10 minutes, or until edges are lightly browned. Remove immediately.

Makes about 7 dozen cookies

Maple Raisin Cookies

HONEY OF A COOKIE

These golden cookies blend popular flavors of honey and carrot into a moist, chewy cookie.

2½ cups all-purpose flour
1 cup sugar
⅔ cup LAND O LAKES® Butter
2 eggs
¼ cup honey
2 teaspoons baking powder

½ teaspoon pumpkin pie spice
¼ teaspoon salt
1 teaspoon vanilla
½ cup shredded carrot (about 1 medium)

Heat oven to 325°. In large mixer bowl, combine flour, sugar, butter, eggs, honey, baking powder, pumpkin pie spice, salt and vanilla. Beat at low speed, scraping bowl often, until well mixed, 2 to 3 minutes. Stir in carrot. Shape rounded teaspoonfuls of dough into 1-inch balls. Place 2 inches apart on ungreased cookie sheets. Bake for 13 to 18 minutes, or until edges are lightly browned. Remove immediately.   *Makes about 4 dozen cookies*

SPICED MOLASSES COOKIES

The old-fashioned flavor of molasses is revived in these spicy, chewy cookies.

2¼ cups all-purpose flour
1 cup sugar
½ cup LAND O LAKES® Butter, softened
½ cup light molasses
¼ cup milk

1 egg
½ teaspoon baking soda
½ teaspoon ground ginger
¼ teaspoon ground cinnamon
⅛ teaspoon salt
Sugar for rolling

In large mixer bowl, combine flour, 1 cup sugar, butter, molasses, milk, egg, baking soda, ginger, cinnamon and salt. Beat at low speed, scraping bowl often, until well mixed, 2 to 3 minutes. Cover; refrigerate until firm, at least 2 hours.

Heat oven to 350°. Shape rounded teaspoonfuls of dough into 1-inch balls. Roll in sugar. Place 2 inches apart on ungreased cookie sheets. Bake for 10 to 12 minutes, or until slightly firm to the touch. Remove immediately.
Makes about 4½ dozen cookies

Honey of a Cookie; Spiced Molasses Cookies

CHOCOLATE MERINGUE PEANUT SQUARES

These one-bake bars have a shortbread crust that is topped with a chocolate peanut meringue.

Crust
1½ cups all-purpose flour
½ cup sugar
¾ cup LAND O LAKES® Butter, softened
2 egg yolks, reserve egg whites
2 teaspoons vanilla

Filling
2 reserved egg whites
⅓ cup sugar
1 cup chopped salted peanuts
½ cup milk chocolate chips

Heat oven to 325°. For crust, in large mixer bowl, combine all crust ingredients. Beat at low speed, scraping bowl often, until mixture is crumbly, 1 to 2 minutes. Press onto bottom of greased 13×9×2-inch baking pan.

For filling, in small bowl, beat egg whites at high speed, scraping bowl often, until soft mounds form, 1 to 2 minutes. Gradually add sugar; beat until stiff peaks form, 1 to 2 minutes. Fold in peanuts and chocolate chips. Spread over crust. Bake for 30 to 35 minutes, or until lightly browned. Cool completely. Cut into squares.   *Makes about 3 dozen squares*

BLACK WALNUT REFRIGERATOR COOKIES

Black walnuts bring a unique flavor to buttery sliced cookies.

3 cups all-purpose flour
1 cup firmly packed brown sugar
1 cup LAND O LAKES® Butter, softened
2 eggs

1 teaspoon baking soda
1 teaspoon cream of tartar
¼ teaspoon salt
1 teaspoon vanilla
1 cup chopped black walnuts

In large mixer bowl, combine flour, sugar, butter, eggs, baking soda, cream of tartar, salt and vanilla. Beat at low speed, scraping bowl often, until well mixed, 3 to 4 minutes. Stir in nuts. Divide dough into halves. Shape each half into a 12×2-inch roll. Wrap in waxed paper; refrigerate until firm, at least 2 hours.

Heat oven to 350°. Cut rolls into ¼-inch slices. Place 1 inch apart on ungreased cookie sheets. Bake for 9 to 12 minutes, or until lightly browned. Remove immediately.   *Makes about 8 dozen cookies*

Chocolate Meringue Peanut Squares

CHOCOLATE PIXIES

These chocolate cookies' powdered sugar coating forms a unique crinkled design during baking.

¼ cup LAND O LAKES® Butter	*4 eggs*
4 squares (1 ounce each)	*2 teaspoons baking powder*
unsweetened chocolate	*½ teaspoon salt*
2 cups all-purpose flour,	*½ cup chopped walnuts or*
divided	*pecans*
2 cups granulated sugar	*Powdered sugar for rolling*

In small saucepan, melt butter and chocolate over low heat, 8 to 10 minutes. Cool. In large mixer bowl, combine melted chocolate mixture, 1 cup of the flour, granulated sugar, eggs, baking powder and salt. Beat at medium speed, scraping bowl often, until well mixed, 2 to 3 minutes. Stir in remaining 1 cup flour and the nuts. Cover; refrigerate until firm, at least 2 hours.

Heat oven to 300°. Shape rounded teaspoonfuls of dough into 1-inch balls; roll in powdered sugar. Place 2 inches apart on greased cookie sheets. Bake for 12 to 15 minutes, or until firm to the touch. Remove immediately.

Makes about 4 dozen cookies

LEMON-BUTTER SNOWBARS

These classic, buttery lemon bars are an all-time favorite.

Crust	**Filling**
1⅓ cups all-purpose flour	*¾ cup granulated sugar*
¼ cup granulated sugar	*2 eggs*
½ cup LAND O LAKES® Butter,	*2 tablespoons all-purpose flour*
softened	*¼ teaspoon baking powder*
	3 tablespoons lemon juice
	Powdered sugar for
	sprinkling

Heat oven to 350°. For crust, in small mixer bowl, combine all crust ingredients. Beat at low speed, scraping bowl often, until mixture is crumbly, 2 to 3 minutes. Press on bottom of ungreased 8-inch square baking pan. Bake for 15 to 20 minutes, or until edges are lightly browned.

For filling, in small mixer bowl, combine granulated sugar, eggs, flour, baking powder and lemon juice. Beat at low speed, scraping bowl often, until well mixed, 1 to 2 minutes. Pour over hot crust. Continue baking for 18 to 20 minutes, or until filling is set. Sprinkle with powdered sugar; cool completely. Cut into bars.

Makes 16 bars

Chocolate Pixies; Lemon-Butter Snowbars

BUTTERY BUTTERSCOTCH CUTOUTS

This buttery cookie has melted butterscotch stirred in for that special flavor.

3 cups all-purpose flour	1 egg
1 cup butterscotch chips, melted	2 tablespoons milk
½ cup granulated sugar	2 teaspoons vanilla
½ cup firmly packed brown sugar	Powdered sugar for sprinkling
1 cup LAND O LAKES® Butter, softened	

In large mixer bowl, combine flour, melted butterscotch chips, granulated sugar, brown sugar, butter, egg, milk and vanilla. Beat at low speed, scraping bowl often, until well mixed, 1 to 2 minutes. Divide dough into halves. Wrap in waxed paper; refrigerate until firm, 1 to 2 hours.

Heat oven to 375°. Roll out dough on well-floured surface to ⅛-inch thickness. Cut out with 2½-inch cookie cutter. Place 1 inch apart on ungreased cookie sheets. Bake for 5 to 8 minutes, or until edges are lightly browned. Remove immediately; cool completely. Sprinkle with powdered sugar or decorate as desired.   *Makes about 4 dozen cookies*

CINNAMON RAISIN OATMEAL COOKIES

These old-fashioned raisin-oatmeal-spice cookies will be a cookie jar favorite.

3 cups quick-cooking oats	1 teaspoon baking soda
2 cups firmly packed brown sugar	1 teaspoon ground cinnamon
1 cup LAND O LAKES® Butter, softened	½ teaspoon salt
2 eggs	2 teaspoons vanilla
	1½ cups all-purpose flour
	1½ cups raisins

Heat oven to 375°. In large mixer bowl, combine oats, sugar, butter, eggs, baking soda, cinnamon, salt and vanilla. Beat at low speed, scraping bowl often, until well mixed, 1 to 2 minutes. Stir in flour until well mixed, 1 to 2 minutes. Stir in raisins. Drop rounded teaspoonfuls of dough 2 inches apart onto greased cookie sheets. Bake for 8 to 10 minutes, or until edges are lightly browned. Remove immediately.   *Makes about 4 dozen cookies*

Buttery Butterscotch Cutouts

LEMON-NUT COOKIES

A rich butter cookie that is lightly flavored with lemon and has the crunch of pecans.

2¾ cups all-purpose flour	½ teaspoon cream of tartar
1½ cups sugar	½ teaspoon salt
¾ cup LAND O LAKES® Butter, softened	2 tablespoons lemon juice
	1 tablespoon grated lemon peel
2 eggs	2 teaspoons vanilla
1 teaspoon baking soda	1 cup chopped pecans

Heat oven to 400°. In large mixer bowl, combine flour, sugar, butter, eggs, baking soda, cream of tartar, salt, lemon juice, lemon peel and vanilla. Beat at low speed, scraping bowl often, until well mixed, 2 to 3 minutes. Stir in nuts. Shape rounded teaspoonfuls of dough into 1-inch balls. Place 2 inches apart on ungreased cookie sheets. Bake for 8 to 10 minutes, or until edges are lightly browned. Remove immediately. *Makes about 4 dozen cookies*

SOUR CREAM BROWN BUTTER COOKIES

Sour cream and brown butter frosting make these moist, tender cookies extra delicious.

Cookies	2 teaspoons vanilla
2⅓ cups all-purpose flour	½ cup chopped pecans
1½ cups granulated sugar	1 cup dairy sour cream
½ cup LAND O LAKES® Butter, softened	
	Frosting
2 eggs	½ cup LAND O LAKES® Butter
1 teaspoon baking soda	2 cups powdered sugar
½ teaspoon baking powder	2 to 3 tablespoons water
½ teaspoon salt	1 teaspoon vanilla

Heat oven to 350°. For cookies, in large mixer bowl, combine flour, granulated sugar, butter, eggs, baking soda, baking powder, salt and vanilla. Beat at low speed, scraping bowl often, until well mixed, 2 to 3 minutes. Stir in nuts and sour cream. Drop rounded teaspoonfuls of dough 2 inches apart onto greased cookie sheets. Bake for 8 to 12 minutes, or until edges are lightly browned. Remove immediately; cool completely.

For frosting, in heavy, small saucepan melt butter, stirring constantly, over low heat until butter is golden brown, 3 to 5 minutes. Stir in remaining ingredients until smooth. Spread over cooled cookies.

Makes about 5 dozen cookies

Lemon-Nut Cookies

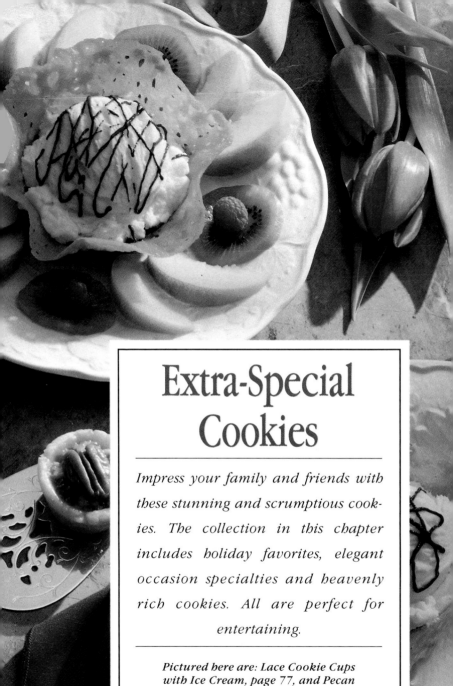

Extra-Special Cookies

Impress your family and friends with these stunning and scrumptious cookies. The collection in this chapter includes holiday favorites, elegant occasion specialties and heavenly rich cookies. All are perfect for entertaining.

Pictured here are: Lace Cookie Cups with Ice Cream, page 77, and Pecan Tartlets, page 78.

ALMOND BRICKLE SUGAR COOKIES

These tender butter cookies can be made two ways.

2¼ cups all-purpose flour
1 cup sugar
1 cup LAND O LAKES® Butter,
   softened
1 egg

1 teaspoon baking soda
1 teaspoon vanilla
1 package (6 ounces) almond
   brickle bits*

Heat oven to 350°. In large mixer bowl, combine flour, sugar, butter, egg, baking soda and vanilla. Beat at medium speed, scraping bowl often, until well mixed, 2 to 3 minutes. Stir in almond brickle bits. Shape rounded teaspoonfuls of dough into 1-inch balls. Place 2 inches apart on greased cookie sheets. Flatten cookies to ¼-inch thickness with bottom of glass dipped in sugar. Bake for 8 to 11 minutes, or until edges are very lightly browned.   *Makes about 4 dozen cookies*

You may substitute 1 cup mini semi-sweet chocolate chips for the almond brickle bits.

LACE COOKIE CUPS WITH ICE CREAM

*Make cookie cups a day ahead. Just before serving
fill and drizzle with chocolate.*

½ cup light corn syrup
½ cup LAND O LAKES® Butter
1 cup all-purpose flour
½ cup firmly packed brown
   sugar

½ cup slivered almonds, finely
   chopped
Semi-sweet chocolate chips,
   melted
Favorite ice cream

Heat oven to 300°. In medium saucepan, bring corn syrup to a full boil over medium heat, 2 to 3 minutes. Add butter; reduce heat to low. Cook, stirring occasionally, until butter melts, 3 to 5 minutes. Remove from heat. Stir in flour, sugar and nuts. Drop tablespoonfuls of dough 4 inches apart onto greased cookie sheets. Bake for 11 to 13 minutes, or until cookies bubble and are golden brown. Cool 1 minute on cookie sheet. Working quickly, remove and shape cookies over inverted small custard cups to form cups. Cool completely; remove from custard cups.

For each cup, spread 1 tablespoon melted chocolate on outside bottom and 1 inch up outside edge of each cooled cup. Refrigerate until chocolate is hardened, about 30 minutes. Just before serving, fill each cup with a large scoop of ice cream. If desired, drizzle with additional melted chocolate.
                        Makes about 2 dozen cookie cups

Almond Brickle Sugar Cookies

TEA-TIME SANDWICH COOKIES

Cookies
2 cups all-purpose flour
1 cup LAND O LAKES® Butter,
  softened
⅓ cup whipping cream
Granulated sugar for dipping

Filling
¾ cup powdered sugar
¼ cup LAND O LAKES® Butter,
  softened
1 to 3 teaspoons milk
1 teaspoon vanilla extract
Food coloring (optional)

For cookies, in small mixer bowl, combine flour, butter and whipping cream. Beat at low speed, scraping bowl often, until well mixed, 2 to 3 minutes. Divide dough into thirds. Wrap in waxed paper. Refrigerate until firm.

Heat oven to 375°. Roll out each ⅓ of the dough on well-floured surface to ⅛-inch thickness. Cut out with 1½-inch round cookie cutters. Dip both sides of each cookie in granulated sugar. Place 1 inch apart on ungreased cookie sheets. Prick with fork. Bake for 6 to 9 minutes, or until slightly puffy but not brown. Cool 1 minute on cookie sheet; remove.

For filling, in small mixer bowl, combine powdered sugar, butter, milk and vanilla. Beat at medium speed, scraping bowl often, until smooth, 1 to 2 minutes. Color filling. Spread ½ teaspoon of filling over bottoms of ½ of the cookies. Top with remaining cookies.   *Makes about 4½ dozen cookies*

PECAN TARTLETS

Bite-size shortbread tarts filled with caramel and pecans.

Tart Shells
½ cup LAND O LAKES® Butter,
  softened
½ cup granulated sugar
1 egg
1 teaspoon almond extract
1¾ cups all-purpose flour

Filling
1 cup powdered sugar
½ cup LAND O LAKES® Butter
⅓ cup dark corn syrup
1 cup chopped pecans
36 pecan halves

Heat oven to 400°. For tart shells, in large mixer bowl, combine all tart shell ingredients. Beat at medium speed, scraping bowl often, until mixture is crumbly, 2 to 3 minutes. Press 1 tablespoon of the mixture into ungreased cups of mini-muffin pans to form 36 (1¾- to 2-inch) shells. Bake for 7 to 10 minutes, or until very lightly browned. Remove from oven.

Reduce oven to 350°. For filling, in medium saucepan, combine powdered sugar, butter and corn syrup. Cook, stirring occasionally, over medium heat until mixture comes to a full boil, 4 to 5 minutes. Remove from heat; stir in chopped nuts. Spoon into baked shells. Top each with pecan half. Bake for 5 minutes. Cool completely; remove.   *Makes about 3 dozen tartlets*

Tea-Time Sandwich Cookies

STRAWBERRY MARZIPAN BARS

Crust
1¼ cups all-purpose flour
⅓ cup firmly packed brown
sugar
½ cup LAND O LAKES® Butter,
softened

Filling
½ cup all-purpose flour
½ cup packed brown sugar
¼ cup LAND O LAKES® Butter,
softened
½ teaspoon almond extract
¾ cup strawberry preserves

Glaze
½ cup powdered sugar
1 to 2 teaspoons milk
½ teaspoon almond extract

Heat oven to 350°. For crust, in small mixer bowl, combine all crust ingredients. Beat at low speed, scraping bowl often, until mixture is crumbly, 1 to 2 minutes. Press on bottom of greased and floured 9-inch square baking pan. Bake for 15 to 20 minutes, or until edges are lightly browned.

For filling, in same mixer bowl, combine flour, brown sugar, butter and almond extract. Beat at low speed, scraping bowl often, until well mixed, 1 to 2 minutes. Spread preserves to within ¼ inch of edge of hot crust. Sprinkle filling mixture over preserves. Continue baking for 20 to 25 minutes, or until edges are lightly browned. Cool completely.

For glaze, in small bowl, stir together all glaze ingredients until smooth. Drizzle over cooled bars. Cut into bars. *Makes about 3 dozen bars*

EGGNOG SNICKERDOODLES

Cookies
2¾ cups all-purpose flour
1½ cups sugar
1 cup LAND O LAKES® Butter,
softened
2 eggs
2 teaspoons cream of tartar
1 teaspoon baking soda

¼ teaspoon salt
½ teaspoon brandy extract
½ teaspoon rum extract

Sugar Mixture
¼ cup sugar or colored sugar
1 teaspoon nutmeg

Heat oven to 400°. For cookies, in large mixer bowl, combine all cookie ingredients. Beat at low speed, scraping bowl often, until well mixed.

For sugar mixture, in small bowl, stir together sugar and nutmeg. Shape rounded teaspoonfuls of dough into 1-inch balls; roll in sugar mixture. Place 2 inches apart on ungreased cookie sheets. Bake for 8 to 10 minutes, or until edges are lightly browned. Remove. *Makes about 4 dozen cookies*

Strawberry Marzipan Bars

ORANGE BUTTER CREAM SQUARES

Crust
1¼ cups finely crushed chocolate
    wafer cookies
⅓ cup LAND O LAKES® Butter,
    softened

Filling
1½ cups powdered sugar
⅓ cup LAND O LAKES® Butter,
    softened
1 tablespoon milk
2 teaspoons grated orange peel
½ teaspoon vanilla

Glaze
1 tablespoon unsweetened
    cocoa
1 tablespoon LAND O LAKES®
    Butter, melted

For crust, in medium bowl, stir together cookie crumbs and butter. Press on bottom of ungreased 9-inch square baking pan. Refrigerate until firm.

For filling, in small mixer bowl, combine all filling ingredients. Beat at medium speed; scrape bowl often until light and fluffy. Spread over crust.

For glaze, in small bowl, stir together cocoa and butter. Drizzle over filling. Refrigerate until firm, about 2 hours. Cut into squares. Store in refrigerator.

Makes about 2 dozen squares

PECAN PIE BARS

Crust
2 cups all-purpose flour
½ cup powdered sugar
1 cup LAND O LAKES® Butter

Filling
1 can (14 ounces) sweetened
    condensed milk
1 egg
1 teaspoon vanilla
1 package (6 ounces) almond
    brickle bits
1 cup chopped pecans

Heat oven to 350°. For crust, in large bowl, combine flour and powdered sugar. Cut in butter until crumbly. Press firmly on bottom of ungreased 13×9×2-inch baking pan. Bake for 15 minutes.

For filling, in large bowl, stir together sweetened condensed milk, egg and vanilla. Stir in almond brickle bits and nuts. Spread evenly over hot crust. Continue baking for 25 to 28 minutes, or until golden brown. Cool; refrigerate until firm, 2 to 3 hours. Cut into bars. Store, covered, in refrigerator.

Makes about 3 dozen bars

Orange Butter Cream Squares

DOUBLE MINT CHOCOLATE COOKIES

Cookies
- 2 cups granulated sugar
- 1 cup unsweetened cocoa
- 1 cup LAND O LAKES® Butter, softened
- 1 cup buttermilk or sour milk
- 1 cup water
- 2 eggs
- 2 teaspoons baking soda
- 1 teaspoon baking powder
- ½ teaspoon salt
- 1 teaspoon vanilla
- 4 cups all-purpose flour

Frosting
- 4 cups powdered sugar
- 1 cup LAND O LAKES® Butter, softened
- 1 teaspoon salt
- 2 tablespoons milk
- 2 teaspoons vanilla
- ½ teaspoon mint extract
- ½ cup crushed starlight peppermint candy

Heat oven to 400°. For cookies, in large mixer bowl, combine granulated sugar, cocoa, butter, buttermilk, water, eggs, baking soda, baking powder, salt and vanilla. Beat at low speed, scraping bowl often, until well mixed, 1 to 2 minutes. Stir in flour until well mixed, 3 to 4 minutes. Drop rounded teaspoonfuls of dough 2 inches apart onto greased cookie sheets. Bake for 7 to 9 minutes, or until top of cookie springs back when touched lightly in center. Remove immediately; cool completely.

For frosting, in small mixer bowl, combine powdered sugar, butter, salt, milk, vanilla and mint extract. Beat at medium speed, scraping bowl often, until light and fluffy, 2 to 3 minutes. Spread ½ tablespoonful of frosting on each cookie. Sprinkle with candy.   *Makes about 8 dozen cookies*

CHERRY JEWELS

These pink molded cookies are buttery rich and very festive.

- 2¼ cups all-purpose flour
- ½ cup granulated sugar
- ⅔ cup LAND O LAKES® Butter, softened
- 1 egg
- ½ teaspoon ground nutmeg
- ¼ teaspoon salt
- ½ teaspoon brandy extract
- ½ cup chopped maraschino cherries, drained
- Powdered sugar for sprinkling

Heat oven to 350°. In large mixer bowl, combine flour, granulated sugar, butter, egg, nutmeg, salt, brandy extract and cherries. Beat at low speed, scraping bowl often, until well mixed, 2 to 3 minutes. Shape rounded teaspoonfuls of dough into 1-inch balls. Place 2 inches apart on ungreased cookie sheets. Bake for 10 to 15 minutes, or until edges are lightly browned. Remove immediately; cool completely. Sprinkle with powdered sugar.
Makes about 3½ dozen cookies

Double Mint Chocolate Cookies

MINT PASTRY WAFERS

2 cups all-purpose flour
1 cup LAND O LAKES® Butter,
    softened
⅓ cup whipping cream or half
    and half

Sugar
24 thin chocolate mint wafers*
    or milk chocolate squares

In large mixer bowl, combine flour, butter and whipping cream. Beat at low speed, scraping bowl often, until well mixed, 1 to 2 minutes. Cover; refrigerate until firm enough to roll, 1 to 2 hours.

Heat oven to 400°. Roll out dough, ½ at a time, on well-floured surface, to ¼-inch thickness. Cut out with 2-inch round cookie cutters. Dip both sides of each cookie in sugar. Place ½ of the cookies 2 inches apart onto greased cookie sheets. Place 1 mint in center of each. Top with another cookie; press together around edges with fingers. Bake for 8 to 10 minutes, or until edges are very lightly browned. Cool 1 minute on cookie sheet; remove.

Makes about 2 dozen cookies

Do not use chocolate fondant mints (cream filled mints).

BITS O'CHOCOLATE BANANA BARS

Bars
2¾ cups all-purpose flour
1¼ cups granulated sugar
1¼ cups bananas cut into ¼-inch
    slices (about 2 large)
¾ cup LAND O LAKES® Butter,
    softened
2 eggs
1¼ teaspoons baking powder
1¼ teaspoons baking soda
½ teaspoon salt

2 teaspoons vanilla
1 cup milk chocolate chips

Frosting
4 cups powdered sugar
½ cup LAND O LAKES® Butter,
    softened
¼ cup milk
2 teaspoons vanilla
    Milk chocolate, shaved into
    small pieces

Heat oven to 350°. For bars, in large mixer bowl, combine flour, granulated sugar, bananas, butter, eggs, baking powder, baking soda, salt and vanilla. Beat at low speed, scraping bowl often, until well mixed, 2 to 3 minutes. Stir in chocolate chips. Spread into greased and floured 15×10×1-inch jelly-roll pan. Bake for 25 to 30 minutes, or until wooden pick inserted in center comes out clean. Cool completely.

For frosting, in mixer bowl, combine powdered sugar, butter, milk and vanilla. Beat at medium speed, scraping bowl often, until light and fluffy. Frost bars. Sprinkle shaved chocolate over tops.   *Makes about 4 dozen bars*

Mint Pastry Wafers

HALF-HEARTED VALENTINE COOKIES

Cookies
¾ cup sugar
1 cup LAND O LAKES® Butter,
   softened
1 package (3 ounces) cream
   cheese, softened
1 egg

1 teaspoon peppermint extract
3 cups all-purpose flour

Glaze
1 cup semi-sweet real chocolate
   chips
¼ cup LAND O LAKES® Butter

For cookies, in large mixer bowl, combine all cookie ingredients except flour. Beat at medium speed, scraping bowl often, until light and fluffy. Add flour; beat until mixed. Divide dough into halves. Wrap in waxed paper. Refrigerate until firm, at least 2 hours.

Heat oven to 375°. Roll out dough on lightly floured surface to ¼-inch thickness. Cut out with floured heart-shaped cutters. Place 1 inch apart on ungreased cookie sheets. Bake for 7 to 10 minutes, or until edges are very lightly browned. Remove immediately; cool completely.

For glaze, in small saucepan, melt chocolate and butter, stirring occasionally, over low heat until melted, 4 to 6 minutes. Dip half of each heart into chocolate. Refrigerate on waxed paper-lined cookie sheet until firm. Store, covered, in refrigerator.   *Makes about 3½ dozen cookies*

LEBKUCHEN SPICE SPRITZ COOKIES

Cookies
⅔ cup granulated sugar
1 cup LAND O LAKES® Butter,
   softened
1 egg
1 teaspoon ground cinnamon
1 teaspoon ground nutmeg
½ teaspoon ground allspice

¼ teaspoon ground cloves
2 teaspoons lemon juice
2 cups all-purpose flour

Glaze
1 cup powdered sugar
1 tablespoon milk
½ teaspoon vanilla

For cookies, in large mixer bowl, combine all cookie ingredients except flour. Beat at medium speed, scraping bowl often, until mixture is light and fluffy. Stir in flour until well mixed. If dough is too soft, cover; refrigerate until firm enough to form cookies.

Heat oven to 400°. Place dough into cookie press; form desired shapes 1 inch apart on greased cookie sheets. Bake for 8 to 12 minutes, or until cookie edges are lightly browned. Remove immediately.

For glaze, in small bowl, stir together all glaze ingredients until smooth. Drizzle glaze on warm cookies.   *Makes about 5 dozen cookies*

Half-Hearted Valentine Cookies

BRANDIED BUTTERY WREATHS

This rich, buttery cookie is delicately flavored with brandy and nutmeg.

Cookies
2¼ cups all-purpose flour
⅓ cup granulated sugar
⅔ cup LAND O LAKES® Butter,
   softened
1 egg
1 teaspoon ground nutmeg
¼ teaspoon salt
2 tablespoons grated orange
   peel
2 tablespoons brandy*
⅓ cup chopped maraschino
   cherries, drained

Glaze
1¼ cups powdered sugar
1 to 2 tablespoons milk
1 tablespoon brandy**
⅛ teaspoon ground nutmeg
Red and green maraschino
   cherries, cut into pieces or
   eighths and drained

Heat oven to 350°. For cookies, in large mixer bowl, combine flour, granulated sugar, butter, egg, nutmeg, salt, orange peel and brandy. Beat at low speed, scraping bowl often, until well mixed, 1 to 2 minutes. Stir in cherries. Shape rounded teaspoonfuls of dough into 1-inch balls; form into 5-inch long strips. Shape strips into circles (wreaths), candy canes or leave as strips. Place 2 inches apart on greased cookie sheets. Bake for 8 to 12 minutes, or until edges are lightly browned. Remove immediately.

For glaze, in small bowl, stir together powdered sugar, milk, brandy and nutmeg until smooth. Frost warm cookies with glaze. Decorate with maraschino cherries.   *Makes about 2 dozen cookies*

*You may substitute 1 teaspoon brandy extract plus 2 tablespoons water for the 2 tablespoons brandy.
**You may substitute ½ teaspoon brandy extract plus 1 tablespoon water for the 1 tablespoon brandy.

Brandied Buttery Wreaths;
Lebkuchen Spice Spritz Cookies, page 89

INDEX

REWARD YOURSELF!
Every time you bake with LAND O LAKES® Butter

That great buttery taste is yours when
you use LAND O LAKES® Butter in these cookie recipes. Super savings can also be yours when
you use LAND O LAKES® Butter proof-of-purchase seals toward popular merchandise from the
Land O'Lakes Catalog. It's our way of rewarding you for being loyal LAND O LAKES® Butter users
over the years. Average savings of over 50% on brands you want, like Corning Ware®, Braun and
Mikasa®. Send for your catalog today!

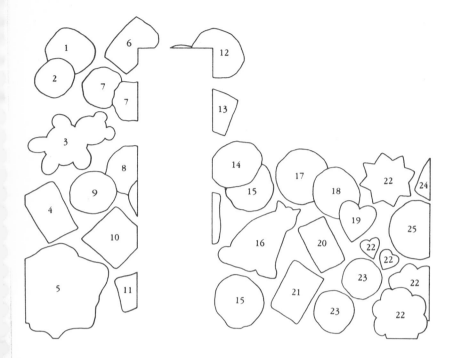

Pictured on front and back cover:

The cookie experts
from Land O'Lakes
invite you to try their
delicious assortment
of melt-in-your
mouth cookies. The
LAND O LAKES®
COOKIE COLLECTION
is a must if you love
cookies. Each bar
cookie, filled cookie,
holiday cookie, drop
cookie and decorated
cookie has been
carefully created
and tested by the
Land O'Lakes Test
Kitchens. And you
can be sure the
buttery goodness of
each LAND O LAKES®
recipe makes every
homemade cookie a
tasty treat.

00382

0 42799 00382 4

ISBN 1-56173-382-2